SIXTEEN SPECTACULAR SMOOTHIES:

KID CREATED AND KID APPROVED

BY KEANE LUDWIG

Copyright © 2024 Keane Ludwig
All rights reserved.
ISBN: **9798874131920**

No duplication without authorization from the author.

INTRODUCTION

I believe eating healthy should be fun and easy! I discovered that eating fruits and vegetables can be very delicious. When I was seven years old, I started creating my own smoothie recipes. By the time I turned nine, I was ready to share sixteen of my favorites. My goal is to empower kids, just like me, to create healthy snacks. This recipe book teaches kids to make healthy snacks for the entire family.

- Each smoothie recipe yields approximately 32-36 ounces, which can be split between you and your family members.
- Choose your favorite type of milk and yogurt. Dairy free options (such as almond, coconut, soy, and cashew) make delicious smoothies!
- Cashew and almond butter may be substituted with your favorite nut butters.

TABLE OF DELICIOUS CONTENTS

1. Banana Berry Bash
2. Banana Berry Go
3. Banana Kiwi Delight
4. Berry Blend
5. Blueberry Banana Bash
6. Cashew Butter Berry Blast
7. Cashew Butter Broccoli
8. Great Grape Delight
9. Mango Berry Blast
10. Maple Mango Mash
11. Melon Berry Blast
12. Peaches and Cream
13. Peach Berry Delight
14. Peach on the Beach
15. Pineapple Spinach Smash
16. Super Spinach Smash

1. BANANA BERRY BASH

Ingredients

- 1 ½ .... bananas
- ¼ cup .... carrots
- 1 cup .... grapes
- ½ cup .... kiwis
- ½ cup .... pineapples
- 1 cup .... blueberries
- ¼ cup .... kale
- 1 cup .... milk

Instructions

1. Add all ingredients to your blender.
2. Place lid on the blender.
3. Plug the blender into the power source.
4. With one hand resting on the lid, turn on your blender.
5. Run the blender for 60 seconds.
6. Turn off the blender.
7. Unplug your blender.
8. Carefully pour smoothie into cups.
9. Sip and enjoy!
10. Share with your family!

2. BANANA BERRY GO

Ingredients

- 1 ½ .... bananas
- 1 cup .... mangoes
- 1 cup .... strawberries
- ½ cup .... blueberries
- ½ cup .... spinach
- 1 cup .... yogurt
- 1 cup .... milk

Instructions

1. Add all ingredients to your blender.
2. Place lid on the blender.
3. Plug the blender into the power source.
4. With one hand resting on the lid, turn on your blender.
5. Run the blender for 60 seconds.
6. Turn off the blender.
7. Unplug your blender.
8. Carefully pour smoothie into cups.
9. Sip and enjoy!
10. Share with your family!

3. Banana Kiwi Delight

Ingredients

- 1 ½ ....bananas
- ½ cup ....blueberries
- ¼ cup ....kale
- ¼ cup ....spinach
- ½ cup ....strawberries
- ½ cup ....grapes
- ½ cup ....pineapple
- 1 cup ....kiwis
- ½ cup ....yogurt
- 1 cup ....milk

Instructions

1. Add all ingredients to your blender.
2. Place lid on the blender.
3. Plug the blender into the power source.
4. With one hand resting on the lid, turn on your blender.
5. Run the blender for 60 seconds.
6. Turn off the blender.
7. Unplug your blender.
8. Carefully pour smoothie into cups.
9. Sip and enjoy!
10. Share with your family!

4. Berry Blend

Ingredients

1 cup.........raspberries
1 cup.........blueberries
1 cup.........blackberries
1 cup.........strawberries
1 cup.........yogurt
1 cup.........milk

Instructions

1. Add all ingredients to your blender.
2. Place lid on the blender.
3. Plug the blender into the power source.
4. With one hand resting on the lid, turn on your blender.
5. Run the blender for 60 seconds.
6. Turn off the blender.
7. Unplug your blender.
8. Carefully pour smoothie into cups.
9. Sip and enjoy!
10. Share with your family!

5. Blueberry Banana Bash

Ingredients

1 ½ ....bananas
½ cup ....mangoes
½ cup ....blueberries
½ cup ....strawberries
½ cup ....spinach
1 cup ....yogurt
1 cup ....milk

Instructions

1. Add all ingredients to your blender.
2. Place lid on the blender.
3. Plug the blender into the power source.
4. With one hand resting on the lid, turn on your blender.
5. Run the blender for 60 seconds.
6. Turn off the blender.
7. Unplug your blender.
8. Carefully pour smoothie into cups.
9. Sip and enjoy!
10. Share with your family!

6. Cashew Butter Berry Blast

Ingredients

- 1 ½ bananas
- ¼ cup cashew butter
- ½ cup blueberries
- ¼ cup broccoli
- ¼ cup spinach
- 1 cup yogurt
- ½ cup orange juice
- ½ cup apple juice
- ½ tbsp lemon juice

Instructions

1. Add all ingredients to your blender.
2. Place lid on the blender.
3. Plug the blender into the power source.
4. With one hand resting on the lid, turn on your blender.
5. Run the blender for 60 seconds.
6. Turn off the blender.
7. Unplug your blender.
8. Carefully pour smoothie into cups.
9. Sip and enjoy!
10. Share with your family!

7. Cashew Butter Broccoli

Ingredients

- 1 .... banana
- ½ cup .... cashew butter
- 1 cup .... blueberries
- ¼ cup .... broccoli
- ¼ cup .... spinach
- 2 cups .... yogurt

Instructions

1. Add all ingredients to your blender.
2. Place lid on the blender.
3. Plug the blender into the power source.
4. With one hand resting on the lid, turn on your blender.
5. Run the blender for 60 seconds.
6. Turn off the blender.
7. Unplug your blender.
8. Carefully pour smoothie into cups.
9. Sip and enjoy!
10. Share with your family!

8. GREAT GRAPE DELIGHT

Ingredients

1 ½ .... bananas
1 cup .... kiwis
1 cup .... grapes
1 cup .... pineapples
1 cup .... yogurt
1 cup .... milk

Instructions

1. Add all ingredients to your blender.
2. Place lid on the blender.
3. Plug the blender into the power source.
4. With one hand resting on the lid, turn on your blender.
5. Run the blender for 60 seconds.
6. Turn off the blender.
7. Unplug your blender.
8. Carefully pour smoothie into cups.
9. Sip and enjoy!
10. Share with your family!

9. Mango Berry Blast

Ingredients

- 1 cup.........strawberries
- 1 cup.........mangoes
- ½ cup ....kiwis
- ½ cup ....blueberries
- ½ cup ....blackberries
- ½ cup ....pineapples
- ¼ cup ....cucumbers
- ¼ cup ....celery
- ¼ cup ....kale
- 2 cups ....apple juice
- 1 tbsp ....lemon juice

Instructions

1. Add all ingredients to your blender.
2. Place lid on the blender.
3. Plug the blender into the power source.
4. With one hand resting on the lid, turn on your blender.
5. Run the blender for 60 seconds.
6. Turn off the blender.
7. Unplug your blender.
8. Carefully pour smoothie into cups.
9. Sip and enjoy!
10. Share with your family!

10. Maple Mango Mash

Ingredients

- 1 ½ .... bananas
- 2 cups .... mangoes
- ¼ cup .... real maple syrup
- 2 cups .... milk

Instructions

1. Add all ingredients to your blender.
2. Place lid on the blender.
3. Plug the blender into the power source.
4. With one hand resting on the lid, turn on your blender.
5. Run the blender for 60 seconds.
6. Turn off the blender.
7. Unplug your blender.
8. Carefully pour smoothie into cups.
9. Sip and enjoy!
10. Share with your family!

Sixteen Spectacular Smoothies:

Kid Created and Kid Approved

by Keane Ludwig

Copyright © 2024 Keane Ludwig
All rights reserved.
ISBN: **9798874131920**

No duplication without authorization from the author.

INTRODUCTION

I believe eating healthy should be fun and easy! I discovered that eating fruits and vegetables can be very delicious. When I was seven years old, I started creating my own smoothie recipes. By the time I turned nine, I was ready to share sixteen of my favorites. My goal is to empower kids, just like me, to create healthy snacks. This recipe book teaches kids to make healthy snacks for the entire family.

- Each smoothie recipe yields approximately 32-36 ounces, which can be split between you and your family members.
- Choose your favorite type of milk and yogurt. Dairy free options (such as almond, coconut, soy, and cashew) make delicious smoothies!
- Cashew and almond butter may be substituted with your favorite nut butters.

Table of Delicious Contents

1. Banana Berry Bash
2. Banana Berry Go
3. Banana Kiwi Delight
4. Berry Blend
5. Blueberry Banana Bash
6. Cashew Butter Berry Blast
7. Cashew Butter Broccoli
8. Great Grape Delight
9. Mango Berry Blast
10. Maple Mango Mash
11. Melon Berry Blast
12. Peaches and Cream
13. Peach Berry Delight
14. Peach on the Beach
15. Pineapple Spinach Smash
16. Super Spinach Smash

1. BANANA BERRY BASH

Ingredients

- 1 ½ .... bananas
- ¼ cup .... carrots
- 1 cup .... grapes
- ½ cup .... kiwis
- ½ cup .... pineapples
- 1 cup .... blueberries
- ¼ cup .... kale
- 1 cup .... milk

Instructions

1. Add all ingredients to your blender.
2. Place lid on the blender.
3. Plug the blender into the power source.
4. With one hand resting on the lid, turn on your blender.
5. Run the blender for 60 seconds.
6. Turn off the blender.
7. Unplug your blender.
8. Carefully pour smoothie into cups.
9. Sip and enjoy!
10. Share with your family!

2. BANANA BERRY GO

Ingredients

    1 ½ .... bananas
    1 cup .... mangoes
    1 cup .... strawberries
    ½ cup .... blueberries
    ½ cup .... spinach
    1 cup .... yogurt
    1 cup .... milk

Instructions

1. Add all ingredients to your blender.
2. Place lid on the blender.
3. Plug the blender into the power source.
4. With one hand resting on the lid, turn on your blender.
5. Run the blender for 60 seconds.
6. Turn off the blender.
7. Unplug your blender.
8. Carefully pour smoothie into cups.
9. Sip and enjoy!
10. Share with your family!

3. Banana Kiwi Delight

Ingredients

1 ½ .... bananas
½ cup .... blueberries
¼ cup .... kale
¼ cup .... spinach
½ cup .... strawberries
½ cup .... grapes
½ cup .... pineapple
1 cup .... kiwis
½ cup .... yogurt
1 cup .... milk

Instructions

1. Add all ingredients to your blender.
2. Place lid on the blender.
3. Plug the blender into the power source.
4. With one hand resting on the lid, turn on your blender.
5. Run the blender for 60 seconds.
6. Turn off the blender.
7. Unplug your blender.
8. Carefully pour smoothie into cups.
9. Sip and enjoy!
10. Share with your family!

4. Berry Blend

Ingredients

1 cup.........raspberries
1 cup.........blueberries
1 cup.........blackberries
1 cup.........strawberries
1 cup.........yogurt
1 cup.........milk

Instructions

1. Add all ingredients to your blender.
2. Place lid on the blender.
3. Plug the blender into the power source.
4. With one hand resting on the lid, turn on your blender.
5. Run the blender for 60 seconds.
6. Turn off the blender.
7. Unplug your blender.
8. Carefully pour smoothie into cups.
9. Sip and enjoy!
10. Share with your family!

5. BLUEBERRY BANANA BASH

Ingredients

- 1 ½ .... bananas
- ½ cup .... mangoes
- ½ cup .... blueberries
- ½ cup .... strawberries
- ½ cup .... spinach
- 1 cup .... yogurt
- 1 cup .... milk

Instructions

1. Add all ingredients to your blender.
2. Place lid on the blender.
3. Plug the blender into the power source.
4. With one hand resting on the lid, turn on your blender.
5. Run the blender for 60 seconds.
6. Turn off the blender.
7. Unplug your blender.
8. Carefully pour smoothie into cups.
9. Sip and enjoy!
10. Share with your family!

6. Cashew Butter Berry Blast

Ingredients

- 1 ½ .... bananas
- ¼ cup .... cashew butter
- ½ cup .... blueberries
- ¼ cup .... broccoli
- ¼ cup .... spinach
- 1 cup .... yogurt
- ½ cup .... orange juice
- ½ cup .... apple juice
- ½ tbsp .... lemon juice

Instructions

1. Add all ingredients to your blender.
2. Place lid on the blender.
3. Plug the blender into the power source.
4. With one hand resting on the lid, turn on your blender.
5. Run the blender for 60 seconds.
6. Turn off the blender.
7. Unplug your blender.
8. Carefully pour smoothie into cups.
9. Sip and enjoy!
10. Share with your family!

7. Cashew Butter Broccoli

Ingredients

- 1 .... banana
- ½ cup .... cashew butter
- 1 cup .... blueberries
- ¼ cup .... broccoli
- ¼ cup .... spinach
- 2 cups .... yogurt

Instructions

1. Add all ingredients to your blender.
2. Place lid on the blender.
3. Plug the blender into the power source.
4. With one hand resting on the lid, turn on your blender.
5. Run the blender for 60 seconds.
6. Turn off the blender.
7. Unplug your blender.
8. Carefully pour smoothie into cups.
9. Sip and enjoy!
10. Share with your family!

8. GREAT GRAPE DELIGHT

Ingredients

1 ½ ....bananas
1 cup.........kiwis
1 cup.........grapes
1 cup.........pineapples
1 cup.........yogurt
1 cup.........milk

Instructions

1. Add all ingredients to your blender.
2. Place lid on the blender.
3. Plug the blender into the power source.
4. With one hand resting on the lid, turn on your blender.
5. Run the blender for 60 seconds.
6. Turn off the blender.
7. Unplug your blender.
8. Carefully pour smoothie into cups.
9. Sip and enjoy!
10. Share with your family!

9. Mango Berry Blast

Ingredients

- 1 cup .... strawberries
- 1 cup .... mangoes
- ½ cup .... kiwis
- ½ cup .... blueberries
- ½ cup .... blackberries
- ½ cup .... pineapples
- ¼ cup .... cucumbers
- ¼ cup .... celery
- ¼ cup .... kale
- 2 cups .... apple juice
- 1 tbsp .... lemon juice

Instructions

1. Add all ingredients to your blender.
2. Place lid on the blender.
3. Plug the blender into the power source.
4. With one hand resting on the lid, turn on your blender.
5. Run the blender for 60 seconds.
6. Turn off the blender.
7. Unplug your blender.
8. Carefully pour smoothie into cups.
9. Sip and enjoy!
10. Share with your family!

10. Maple Mango Mash

Ingredients

- 1 ½ .... bananas
- 2 cups .... mangoes
- ¼ cup .... real maple syrup
- 2 cups .... milk

Instructions

1. Add all ingredients to your blender.
2. Place lid on the blender.
3. Plug the blender into the power source.
4. With one hand resting on the lid, turn on your blender.
5. Run the blender for 60 seconds.
6. Turn off the blender.
7. Unplug your blender.
8. Carefully pour smoothie into cups.
9. Sip and enjoy!
10. Share with your family!

11. Melon Berry Blast

Ingredients

- 1 cup .... watermelon
- ½ cup .... raspberries
- ½ cup .... blueberries
- ½ cup .... blackberries
- ¼ cup .... spinach
- ¼ cup .... kale
- 1 cup .... yogurt

Instructions

1. Add all ingredients to your blender.
2. Place lid on the blender.
3. Plug the blender into the power source.
4. With one hand resting on the lid, turn on your blender.
5. Run the blender for 60 seconds.
6. Turn off the blender.
7. Unplug your blender.
8. Carefully pour smoothie into cups.
9. Sip and enjoy!
10. Share with your family!

12. PEACHES AND CREAM

Ingredients

3 cups .... peaches
1 .... banana
1 cup .... yogurt
1 cup .... milk

Instructions

1. Add all ingredients to your blender.
2. Place lid on the blender.
3. Plug the blender into the power source.
4. With one hand resting on the lid, turn on your blender.
5. Run the blender for 60 seconds.
6. Turn off the blender.
7. Unplug your blender.
8. Carefully pour smoothie into cups.
9. Sip and enjoy!
10. Share with your family!

13. Peach Berry Delight

Ingredients

- 1 cup .... peaches
- 1 cup .... strawberries
- ½ cup .... raspberries
- ½ cup .... blackberries
- ¼ cup .... kale
- ¼ cup .... spinach
- ½ cup .... yogurt
- 1 cup .... milk

Instructions

1. Add all ingredients to your blender.
2. Place lid on the blender.
3. Plug the blender into the power source.
4. With one hand resting on the lid, turn on your blender.
5. Run the blender for 60 seconds.
6. Turn off the blender.
7. Unplug your blender.
8. Carefully pour smoothie into cups.
9. Sip and enjoy!
10. Share with your family!

14. Peach on the Beach

Ingredients

- 1 cup .... peaches
- ½ cup .... almond butter
- ½ cup .... blueberries
- ½ cup .... strawberries
- ¼ cup .... broccoli
- ¼ cup .... carrots
- 2 cups .... milk

Instructions

1. Add all ingredients to your blender.
2. Place lid on the blender.
3. Plug the blender into the power source.
4. With one hand resting on the lid, turn on your blender.
5. Run the blender for 60 seconds.
6. Turn off the blender.
7. Unplug your blender.
8. Carefully pour smoothie into cups.
9. Sip and enjoy!
10. Share with your family!

15. Pineapple Spinach Smash

Ingredients

- 1 cup.........pineapples
- 1 cup.........strawberries
- 1 ....banana
- ½ cup........spinach
- 2 cups ....milk

Instructions

1. Add all ingredients to your blender.
2. Place lid on the blender.
3. Plug the blender into the power source.
4. With one hand resting on the lid, turn on your blender.
5. Run the blender for 60 seconds.
6. Turn off the blender.
7. Unplug your blender.
8. Carefully pour smoothie into cups.
9. Sip and enjoy!
10. Share with your family!

16. Super Spinach Smash

Ingredients

- 1 banana
- 1 cup peaches
- ½ cup kiwis
- ¼ cup spinach
- ¼ cup kale
- 1 cup yogurt
- 1 cup milk

Instructions

1. Add all ingredients to your blender.
2. Place lid on the blender.
3. Plug the blender into the power source.
4. With one hand resting on the lid, turn on your blender.
5. Run the blender for 60 seconds.
6. Turn off the blender.
7. Unplug your blender.
8. Carefully pour smoothie into cups.
9. Sip and enjoy!
10. Share with your family!

Create your own smoothie recipes and write them on the following pages!

Smoothie Name: _____

Ingredients:

- _____
- _____
- _____
- _____
- _____
- _____
- _____
- _____

Instructions:

_____
_____
_____
_____
_____

Smoothie Name: _____

Ingredients:

- _____
- _____
- _____
- _____
- _____
- _____
- _____
- _____

Instructions:

_____
_____
_____
_____
_____

Smoothie Name: _____

Ingredients:

- _____
- _____
- _____
- _____
- _____
- _____
- _____
- _____

Instructions:

_____
_____
_____
_____
_____

Smoothie Name: _____

Ingredients:

- _____
- _____
- _____
- _____
- _____
- _____
- _____
- _____

Instructions:

_____
_____
_____
_____
_____

Smoothie Name: _____

Ingredients:

- _____
- _____
- _____
- _____
- _____
- _____
- _____
- _____

Instructions:

_____
_____
_____
_____
_____

Smoothie Name: _____

Ingredients:

- _____
- _____
- _____
- _____
- _____
- _____
- _____
- _____

Instructions:

_____
_____
_____
_____
_____

Smoothie Name: _____

Ingredients:

- _____
- _____
- _____
- _____
- _____
- _____
- _____
- _____

Instructions:

_____
_____
_____
_____
_____

Smoothie Name: _____

Ingredients:

- _____
- _____
- _____
- _____
- _____
- _____
- _____
- _____

Instructions:

_____
_____
_____
_____
_____

Made in the USA
Middletown, DE
06 February 2025

11. Melon Berry Blast

Ingredients

- 1 cup .... watermelon
- ½ cup .... raspberries
- ½ cup .... blueberries
- ½ cup .... blackberries
- ¼ cup .... spinach
- ¼ cup .... kale
- 1 cup .... yogurt

Instructions

1. Add all ingredients to your blender.
2. Place lid on the blender.
3. Plug the blender into the power source.
4. With one hand resting on the lid, turn on your blender.
5. Run the blender for 60 seconds.
6. Turn off the blender.
7. Unplug your blender.
8. Carefully pour smoothie into cups.
9. Sip and enjoy!
10. Share with your family!

12. PEACHES AND CREAM

Ingredients

   3 cups ....peaches
   1 ....banana
   1 cup.........yogurt
   1 cup.........milk

Instructions

1. Add all ingredients to your blender.
2. Place lid on the blender.
3. Plug the blender into the power source.
4. With one hand resting on the lid, turn on your blender.
5. Run the blender for 60 seconds.
6. Turn off the blender.
7. Unplug your blender.
8. Carefully pour smoothie into cups.
9. Sip and enjoy!
10. Share with your family!

13. Peach Berry Delight

Ingredients

- 1 cup.........peaches
- 1 cup.........strawberries
- ½ cup........raspberries
- ½ cup........blackberries
- ¼ cup........kale
- ¼ cup........spinach
- ½ cup........yogurt
- 1 cup.........milk

Instructions

1. Add all ingredients to your blender.
2. Place lid on the blender.
3. Plug the blender into the power source.
4. With one hand resting on the lid, turn on your blender.
5. Run the blender for 60 seconds.
6. Turn off the blender.
7. Unplug your blender.
8. Carefully pour smoothie into cups.
9. Sip and enjoy!
10. Share with your family!

14. Peach on the Beach

Ingredients

- 1 cup .... peaches
- ½ cup .... almond butter
- ½ cup .... blueberries
- ½ cup .... strawberries
- ¼ cup .... broccoli
- ¼ cup .... carrots
- 2 cups .... milk

Instructions

1. Add all ingredients to your blender.
2. Place lid on the blender.
3. Plug the blender into the power source.
4. With one hand resting on the lid, turn on your blender.
5. Run the blender for 60 seconds.
6. Turn off the blender.
7. Unplug your blender.
8. Carefully pour smoothie into cups.
9. Sip and enjoy!
10. Share with your family!

15. Pineapple Spinach Smash

Ingredients

- 1 cup .... pineapples
- 1 cup .... strawberries
- 1 .... banana
- ½ cup .... spinach
- 2 cups .... milk

Instructions

1. Add all ingredients to your blender.
2. Place lid on the blender.
3. Plug the blender into the power source.
4. With one hand resting on the lid, turn on your blender.
5. Run the blender for 60 seconds.
6. Turn off the blender.
7. Unplug your blender.
8. Carefully pour smoothie into cups.
9. Sip and enjoy!
10. Share with your family!

16. SUPER SPINACH SMASH

Ingredients

- 1 .... banana
- 1 cup .... peaches
- ½ cup .... kiwis
- ¼ cup .... spinach
- ¼ cup .... kale
- 1 cup .... yogurt
- 1 cup .... milk

Instructions

1. Add all ingredients to your blender.
2. Place lid on the blender.
3. Plug the blender into the power source.
4. With one hand resting on the lid, turn on your blender.
5. Run the blender for 60 seconds.
6. Turn off the blender.
7. Unplug your blender.
8. Carefully pour smoothie into cups.
9. Sip and enjoy!
10. Share with your family!

Create your own smoothie recipes and write them on the following pages!

Smoothie Name: _____

Ingredients:

- _____
- _____
- _____
- _____
- _____
- _____
- _____
- _____

Instructions:

_____
_____
_____
_____
_____

Smoothie Name: _____

Ingredients:

- _____
- _____
- _____
- _____
- _____
- _____
- _____
- _____

Instructions:

_____
_____
_____
_____
_____

Smoothie Name: _____

Ingredients:

- _____
- _____
- _____
- _____
- _____
- _____
- _____
- _____

Instructions:

_____
_____
_____
_____
_____

Smoothie Name: _____

Ingredients:

- _____
- _____
- _____
- _____
- _____
- _____
- _____
- _____

Instructions:

_____
_____
_____
_____
_____

Smoothie Name: _____

Ingredients:

- _____
- _____
- _____
- _____
- _____
- _____
- _____
- _____

Instructions:

_____
_____
_____
_____
_____

Smoothie Name: _____

Ingredients:

- _____
- _____
- _____
- _____
- _____
- _____
- _____
- _____

Instructions:

_____
_____
_____
_____
_____

Smoothie Name: _____

Ingredients:

- _____
- _____
- _____
- _____
- _____
- _____
- _____
- _____

Instructions:

_____
_____
_____
_____
_____

Smoothie Name: _____

Ingredients:

- _____
- _____
- _____
- _____
- _____
- _____
- _____
- _____

Instructions:

_____
_____
_____
_____
_____

Made in the USA
Middletown, DE
06 February 2025